THE BULLYING PHENOMENON

Breaking the Cycle

ACTIVITY WORKBOOK

DWAYNE AND TIFFANY RUFFIN

This workbook is dedicated to the memory of Mary R. Ruffin-Thompkins and Tella Williams.

To our children for their love and support and to our fellow educators in whom we stand collectively composed on the front line, eradicating illiteracy and encouraging lifelong learners.

Last, to my armed services comrades, who defend this nation's civil liberties without regard to unimaginable sacrifice.

Copyright © 2019 by Dwayne Ruffin, Ed. D. & Tiffany Ruffin, M.S. All rights reserved. No part of this publication may be reproduced, distributed, or transmitted in any form or by any means, including photocopying, recording, or other electronic or mechanical methods, without the prior written permission of the publisher, except in the case of brief quotations embodied in critical reviews and certain other noncommercial uses permitted by copyright law. No liability is assumed for damages that may result from the use of information contained within. For permission requests, write to the publisher, addressed "Attention: Permissions Coordinator," at the address below.

Trey Nickel Publishing
Lansing, IL 60438

treynickelpublishing@gmail.com

Book design by Cierra Cole Consulting.

Cover image by agefotostock.com

Interior Design by Adept Content Solutions

Manufactured in the United States

ISBN: 978-0-9989023-0-2

LCCN: 2019916001

CONTENTS

K-W-L Chart   *v*
Introduction   *vii*

1. What Is Bullying?   1
2. A Comparison of Bullying and Conflict   3
3. What Are the Orgins of Bullying   5
4. The Mindset of a Bully   11
5. The Bully's Line of Attack   13
6. Why People Bully Others   15
7. What Roles Are Components of Bullying?   19
8. What Are the Types of Bullying?   21
9. Cyberbullying Prevention Guidelines   27
10. What Are the Effects of Bullying?   31
11. What Are the Steps in Dealing with a Bully?   35
12. Be Assertive When Communicating with Bullies   39
13. Bullying Victimization Warning Signs   53
14. Interventions for Bullying and School Violence   55
15. Coping Strategies for Emotional Management   79

Conclusion   *83*
References   *85*
Additional Resources   *88*

K-W-L CHART

Author's note: I'm encouraging your participation as critical thinking readers. Please feel free to copy and utilize the K-W-L chart while reading the text. I anticipate your "ah-ha" moment will come when you're fully engaged in reflection on the content of each chapter.

The K-W-L (Ogle, 1986) chart is a reading strategy that is used to guide readers through a text. First the reader begins by brainstorming everything they Know about the given topic. This information is recorded in the K column of the K-W-L chart. Next as the reader generates a list of questions about what they Want to Know about the topic. These questions are listed in the W column. This new information that they have Learned is recorded in the L column of the K-W-L.

K-W-L ACTIVITY CHART

KNOW	WANT TO KNOW	LEARNED

INTRODUCTION

This workbook can help the reader increase awareness and develop knowledge and skills through experiential learning activities with minimal facilitation, as well boost student engagement and accelerate learning and improve content retention. Students who engage in the learning activities are less likely to become bored and disinterested. Moreover, students involved in the learning process are more likely to become engaged emotionally, which helps them to experience learning in a dynamic way. This will result in learning deep problem-solving and critical thinking skills firsthand.

Bullying is a global antisocial phenomenon that affects adults, the elderly, adolescents, and children. Bullying exists as an egregious, insidious, and antisocial behavior that traumatizes millions of students each year.

The Bullying Phenomenon: Breaking the Cycle gives awareness of bullying rituals and bullying prevention tips and tools as well as effective anti-bullying interventions with emphasis featured in the Bullying Resolution Model that develops Assertiveness, Mediation, Empathy, Accountability, Problem-Solving, Active Listening, and Interviewing Skills through facilitation until resolution is achieved.

The Bullying Phenomenon: Breaking the Cycle is a research and evidence–based guidebook. The guidebook, and now the workbook, use approaches grounded in constructivism, inquiry, reflective, collaborative, and integrative-based curriculum. The authors' first book *The Bullying Phenomenon: Breaking the Cycle* (Ruffin, 2017), coupled with *The Bullying Phenomenon: Breaking the Cycle* activity workbook provides teachers and administrators as well parents and concerned citizens with effective, practical anti-bullying protocols that seek to quell the cycle of bullying—one child, one classroom, and one learning institution at a time.

1. WHAT IS BULLYING?

Bullying is a form of anti-social abuse that repetitively victimizes others over a period. Bullying is an aggressive behavior intended to hurt or harm another person often driven by feelings of anger, revenge, and frustration. Bullying is a form of victimization and cannot be addressed as "conflict" because that downplays the negative behavior and seriousness of the effects. Bullying takes place wherever human interaction occurs, even in your space.

2. A COMPARISON OF BULLYING AND CONFLICT

BULLYING CRITERA VS. CONFLICT CRITERIA

Victimization / Stop behavior

Without justification / Action or expression occurs

Imbalance of power control / Equal power

Manipulate others and situations / Disagreement/arguments

Repeated over time / Poor communication

Audience (never alone) seekers / Care about outcomes

ACTIVITY: BULLYING CRITERIA WORD SEARCH

```
Y A N D Y I M Q X R D D G R N
I N S O W E G L B H U R T K O
N O Y N I T K B Q K O P Q C I
T I S U K T E B Y L T A D Q C
I T X E S C A H T V P E E F R
M A S C P W M C L H R N O S E
I Z E O O T R V I E R V Q W O
D I R N R M A L T F E E N A C
A M U T A G H N D R I H A B Y
T I T R D L E A T T I T F T B
I T S O H C K I S I K Z S G S
O C E L F L M J X U P K P U L
N I G L V E W H V A D R A J J
A V E M A N I P U L A T I O N
Q S P B P E A U D I E N C E G
```

WORD LIST

Audience
Harm
Hurt
Intimidation

Justification
Manipulation
Over Time
Self-centered
Threats

Victimization
Coercion
Control
Gestures

3. WHAT ARE THE ORGINS OF BULLYING?

THE ORGINS OF BULLYING THEORETICAL FRAMEWORK

Systems thinking is a way of approaching dilemmas that asks how an individual occurrence influence another (cause and effect). Rather than reacting to individual behavior that arises, a systems thinker will be mindful of correlations to other behaviors within the system and seek out root causes. In developing the origins of bullying and furthering research, I drew upon Hall's (1976) Cultural Iceberg Model to create a visual rationalization for the origins of bullying.

The iceberg diagram developed serves as a visual aid for readers to understand the origins (envy, pride, greed, rage, apathy, unforgiveness) of bullying. Also, the iceberg diagram gives deep insight into why people behave the way they do.

Bullying behaviors are manifested through jealousy, feeling insecure, and underlying social, emotional, as well as learned behavior, and even physical issues or problems that are concealed but taken out on others. Bullying behavior is an outcry of the nature of man's self-centered and self-serving mindset that is justified through the lust of the eye, lust of the heart, and pride of life: "It's all about me, but not you."

In viewing the diagram, I encourage readers to observe the three baselines of the iceberg model: the tip of the iceberg, the water line, and the hidden depth beneath the surface. Above the iceberg's water line, the viewer can observe the types of bullying abuse (physical, social, cyber, prejudicial, and sexual) that occur throughout episodes of victimization. The external, or conscious, part of bullying culture is what we can see at the tip of the iceberg. Behaviors above the water line include visible aspects of bullying behaviors.

3. WHAT ARE THE ORGINS OF BULLYING? | 7

ICEBERG MODEL

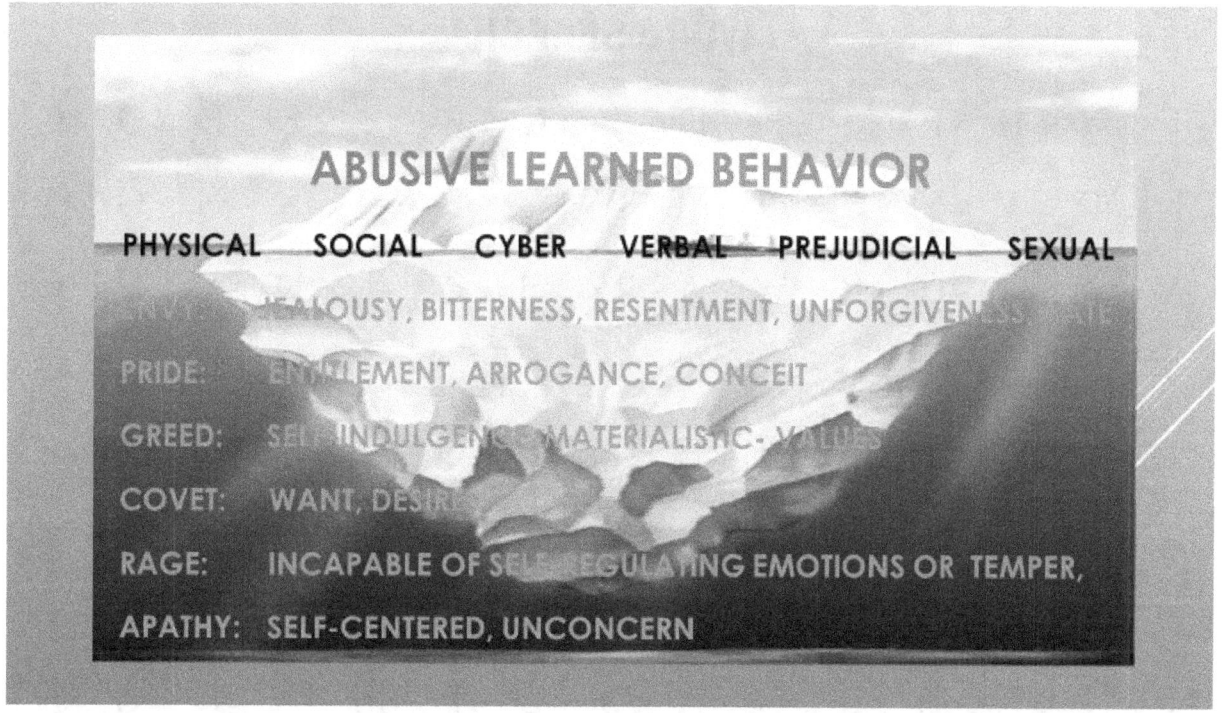

The origins, the internal or subconscious part, of bullying culture is below the larger portion of the water line hidden beneath the surface and includes beliefs, values, pride of life, lust of the spirit, and thought patterns that underlie bullying behaviors.

As stated previously, rather than reacting to individual behavior that arises, a systems thinker (informed school administrator, dean, teacher, counselor) will be mindful of correlations to other behaviors within the system and seek out root causes instead of just addressing the behavior without authentic and meaningful interventions that could lead to systemic transformation.

ACTIVITY: BULLYING ORGINS
WORD SEARCH

```
E Y H F S F D P G R E E D Q C
N D V Y C Q M W Y B N S N O J
V A D G R W A H H G T D V U C
Y A E I U E T Q L O I E B N O
L B R A E N E E F Q T N O F F
Z U E B L M R R C Q L J J O F
F S T E T M I I H F E E I R P
F I N H R Q A S D E M A O G H
N V E A E Y L E D D E L A I O
B E C V A A I D I I N O C V L
G W F I T X S V W R T U Y E C
P A L O M X T F Q P H S U N O
U O E R E Q I W G K T Y P E P
E I S W N I C M J A I C R S P
U R D S T F K A P A T H Y S B
```

WORD LIST

Behavior	Apathy	Unforgiveness
Envy	Desire	Materialistic
Jealousy	Entitlement	Inadequacy
Covert	Abusive	Cruel-Treatment
Rage	Pride	Self-Centered
	Greed	

ACTIVITY: QUESTIONS TO CONSIDER AFTER TRYING OUT THE ICEBERG MODEL

1. Does the iceberg model help broaden your perspective? If so, how might this new perspective be helpful?

   _____

   _____

   _____

2. Leverage points highlight the root causes that influence bullying behavior (hidden beneath the surface). After analyzing the Iceberg Model, list your perceptions of why bullies victimize others.

   _____

   _____

   _____

3. What issues that have frustrated you might be interesting to analyze with the Iceberg Model?

   _____

   _____

   _____

4. THE MINDSET OF A BULLY

The mindset of a bully is determined by fixed mental attitude or disposition that predetermines a person's response to life interpretations of situations. These learned inclinations or habits are embedded in the person's core and even become intense when unresolved desires, experiences, morals, and emotions are not self-regulated.

- They lack appreciation for diversity/uniqueness.
- They have negative perceptions, attitude, self-image, and beliefs.
- They have learning frustration and a lack of classroom productivity.
- They have learned negative behavior from family instability and negative or hurtful memories.

- They have identity crisis and lack of coherent expression of thoughts, ideas, or feelings.
- They lack of social and emotional competency and interactions.
- They never take ownership, acceptance, accountability, and responsibility for behavior and actions.

5. THE BULLY'S LINE OF ATTACK

- threats
- coercion
- intimidation
- cruel treatment
- insulting comments or gesture

6. WHY PEOPLE BULLY OTHERS

Victims are bullied and harassed because they are often viewed as being different. These differences may include obesity, being small in physical stature, or having learning or physical disabilities; students with different sexual orientations as well as emotional deficiencies can also be victimized often by bullying. Some people who dominate others (or want to dominate others) have underlying social, emotional, and even physical issues urging them to control others so that their own inadequacies will not become exposed.

This is an indirect way to make the bully feel better. By degrading the victim with verbal, physical, and emotional abuse, the bully somehow eases his or her own pain though temporarily and superficially. Consequently, the bully attempts to elevate his or her own ego through the degradation of others.

This domineering and sometimes sadistic behavior seem to be genetically predisposed, but ultimately it develops from harsh parenting styles.

- They want to dominate, control, and manipulate.
- They want or need power.
- They want to use embarrassing information.
- They want to maintain personal popularity or get ahead at the expense of others.

6. WHY PEOPLE BULLY OTHERS | 17

ACTIVITY

Name the types of bullying criteria you're experiencing.

_____

_____

_____

Why do you think the bully has chosen you?

_____

_____

_____

Who was the audience when you were victimized by the bully or bullies?

_____

_____

_____

How long have you been abused or victimized by the bully or bullies?

_____

_____

_____

It's not your fault for being victimized by a bully! Go now; identify and expose the bully to an adult, which will cause the bully to lose power!

_____

_____

7. WHAT ROLES ARE COMPONENTS OF BULLYING

★Note: As students attend school, they move in clusters through grade levels, therefore, forming social relationships that consist of all type of personalities. Some students are passive, aggressive, bossy, streetwise, naïve, and even exposed to issues that aren't age appropriate.

Bullying affects the mood, thinking, and behavior of the bully, the victim, and the bystander. Research suggests that bullying usually occurs in the presence of peers who can adopt a variety of roles, such as (a) remaining neutral during a bullying incident; (b) assisting and encouraging the bully; (c) aiding or consoling the victim; or (d) reversing roles by assuming the position as the bully, victim, or bystander.

THE BULLY

Bullying has far-reaching effects on the victim, the bully, and the bystander. Victims of bullying are at increased risk for physical and emotional problems. They are also at risk for becoming a bully.

THE BYSTANDER

In contrast, bystanders are at increased risk for developing depression, anxiety, and not attending school or even dropping out. Bystanders are likely to feel guilt regarding inaction during bullying incidents and recognize how the learning environment and school culture is unsafe.

THE VICTIM

In addition, bullies are at risk for getting into fights as well as committing crimes. In fact, they are more likely to abuse drugs and alcohol as a youth.

8. WHAT ARE THE TYPES OF BULLYING?

PHYSICAL BULLYING involves hurting a person's body or possessions.

- Hitting/kicking/pinching
- Spitting tripping/pushing
- Taking or breaking someone's things
- Making mean or rude hand gestures

VERBAL BULLYING is saying or writing mean things.

- Teasing
- Name-calling
- Inappropriate sexual comments
- Taunting
- Threatening to cause harm

SOCIAL BULLYING is sometimes referred to as relational bullying.

- Involves hurting someone's reputation or relationships
- Leaving someone out on purpose
- Telling other not to be friends with the individual or group
- Spreading rumors about someone or embarrassing someone in public

CYBERBULLYING The most common media for cyberbullying are texting and email through electronic devices (cellular phone, tablets, computers), for example, uploading lewd or offensive pictures and then posting information on social media sites.

8. WHAT ARE THE TYPES OF BULLYING? | 23

ACTIVITY: DEVELOP AN UNDERSTANDING OF BULLYING

Note: As you develop an understanding of bullying, mindsets, components and type, please determine what bullying rituals are embedded within the poem stanza and record your response.

POEM STANZA	CONVEY IN WRITING POEM STANZA MEANING
How much longer can I take, constantly trying not to break; it goes on and on—day by day, another piece of me chiseled away.	
Called names like ugly, strange and fat, how am I meant to put up with that? Why is this happening to me? I ask you nicely set me free!	
My pillow is soaking with all my tears. School always gives me fears. The girls and boys scream and shout, in this cage of worries—let me out.	
I beg for all this hurt to stop. I feel like I'm falling like a raindrop. I don't think I can take much more. Zero to me, one to you—that's the score. I want to go; I want to leave. Let me go, please, oh please. Do you agree life's one big con? Please don't look for me when I'm gone.	

BULLYING VS. CYBERBULLYING COMPARISON CHART

BULLYING	CYBERBULLYING
Direct	Anonymous
Occurs on school property	Occurs off school property
Poor relationship with teachers	Good relationship with teachers
Fear of retribution	Fear of loss of technology privileges
Physical: hitting, pushing shoving **Verbal:** teasing, name calling, gossip **Nonverbal:** use of gestures, and exclusion	Further under the radar than bullying; emotional reaction cannot be determined

CYBERBULLYING STATISTICS

- 75 percent of kids admit someone has said mean or hurtful things to them online and four out ten say it has happened more than once.
- 58 percent of kids have been bullied online.
- 81 percent of young people think bullying online is easier to get away with.
- Girls are about twice as likely as boys to be both victims and perpetrators of cyberbullying.

ACTIVITY: BULLYING TYPES

Directions: Write letter of the answer in Column B that best matches the description in Column A.

COLUMN A	COLUMN B
1. ____ Texting and emailing to victimize	a. Physical Bullying
1. ____ Hurting someone's reputation	b. Verbal Bullying
2. ____ The bystander	c. Social Bullying
3. ____ Teasing	d. Cyberbullying
4. ____ Name-calling	e. Bullying Ritual Elements
5. ____ Leaving someone out on purpose	
6. ____ Spreading rumors about someone	
7. ____ The bully	
8. ____ Spitting tripping/pushing	
9. ____ Breaking someone's things	
10. ____ Making rude gestures	
11. ____ Embarrassing someone in public.	

9. CYBERBULLYING PREVENTION GUIDELINES

- Refuse to pass along cyberbullying messages.
- Tell friends to stop cyberbullying.
- Block communication with cyberbullies.
- Report cyberbullying to a trusted adult.
- Speak with other students, teachers and school administrators to develop rules against cyberbullying.
- Never give out your name or any other personal information, i.e. email and passwords.
- Never send a picture of yourself to a stranger.
- Tell an adult if anyone makes you uncomfortable while online.

ACTIVITY

Describe how people are cyberbullying others.
_____
_____
_____

Which examples in the diagram match your experience with being bullied?
_____
_____
_____

Have you ever informed a parent or trusted adult about online abuse?
_____
_____
_____

What is your response to the statement that girls are about twice as likely as boys to be victims and perpetrators of cyberbullying?
_____
_____
_____

9. CYBERBULLYING PREVENTION GUIDELINES | 29

ACTIVITY

Respond to this question as indicated below.

I've anonymously been bullied by someone and have exchange emails. Can I contact and report the abuse to the content provider?

○ TRUE

○ FALSE

If you or friend is being cyberbullied, first you should notify an adult. Then you should block the bully's communication by blocking their social media profile.

○ TRUE

○ FALSE

When pictures, hurtful remarks, and embarrassing information are posted online, the delete button erases all items posted forever and therefore the following statement is true: 81 percent of young people think bullying online is easier to get away with and can't be tracked by the provider.

○ TRUE

○ FALSE

10. WHAT ARE THE EFFECTS OF BULLYING?

The effects of bullying are well documented and include negative impacts on student development and academic achievement. Bullying, consequently, causes psychological harm as well as a lack of normative social interactions as well as maladaptive outcomes for children who engage in bullying. Moreover, Dake, Price, and Telljohann (2003), noted that the media attention on homicide and suicide cases may point to increases in school bullying.

Meyer-Adams and Conner (2008) suggested that bullying may not only be the precursor of unresolved bullying issues but may also be the outcome of conflicts that escalate to devastating incidents, such as the suicide of Tyler Clementi, a Rutgers University freshman, and Ryan Halligan, a thirteen-year-old boy from Essex Junction, Vermont.

Other examples include the shootings at Blacksburg, Virginia, and Columbine High School in Colorado. At this point within the United States concerns have increased because of high-level violence resulting from representative, well-publicized school shootings occurring in various states, such as Minnesota, Missouri, Virginia, and Ohio.

Other problems include:

- Physical problems (headaches, regurgitating, stomach cramps, eating disorder and loss of appetite).
- Unresolved and suppressed emotional problems (stress, anger, depression, anxieties, or mistrust as well as social phobias).
- Lack of social competency development.
- Withdrawal from friends, loved ones, and social activities.
- Feelings of helplessness or powerlessness.
- Suicidal ideation
- Shootings.
- Assimilation behavior.
- Negative/ hurtful memories.
- Lack of concentration and decline in schoolwork.
- Mood swings.
- Nightmares or problems sleeping.
- Addictive behavior.

ACTIVITY: EFFECTS OF BULLYING WORD SEARCH

```
A S N P P O W E R L E S S A F
S E H O F N A U E L S I E D G
E H W V I C U D A G F M R D I
I C B A M T I W N C E P A I K
T A R O H C A I C R A R M C K
E D H C I R W L W Q S E T T L
I A H U D S M E I K G D H I A
X E S H D J I N H M N R G O N
N H T O S Y S Q S Y I O I N O
A I O W R L T W S E T S N R I
W M R E R O R Q E G O I S N T
Z D U E H M U E R M O D Y A O
N M B Z G Z S O T H H M V J M
F D G I V N T R S T S O N Z E
D L E S E D A R G R O O P V P
```

WORD LIST

Addiction	Mistrust	Mood Swings	Shootings
Anger	Disorder	Nightmares	Stress
Anxieties	Emotional	Poor grades	Suicide
Assimilation	Headaches	Powerless	Withdrawal

Depression

11. WHAT ARE THE STEPS IN DEALING WITH A BULLY?

EXPOSE THE BULLY: Remember, being bullied isn't your fault.

- CONFRONT THE BULLY
  - Don't react to any inappropriate behavior.
  - Mobilize the support of others.
  - Be assertive in conversation.
  - Keep cool and remain calm; bullies seek negative responses.
  - Be mindful and don't respond with anger.

- TELL AN ADULT
  - Cut off the bully's power.
  - Let bullies know their behavior is unacceptable.

- *IGNORE AND AVOID THE BULLY*
  - Block social media profile
  - Do not give in to the bully's demands
  - Don't become isolated

- DOCUMENT INCIDENT
  - Focus on what happened
  - What the person did
  - What the person said
  - Identify the bystanders (witness)
  - Describe how personal contact was made

ACTIVITY: JOURNAL THE INCIDENT

What happened/ What did the person do? What did the person say?

When did it take place (time/ date)?

Where did it take place?

Who was the person?

Who are the bystanders (witness)?

What was your response or action?

Did you report the incident?

GUIDELINES FOR PARENTS, SCHOOL ADMINISTRATORS, TEACHERS, AND CONCERNED CITIZENS

- Stop the bullying immediately.
- Refer to school rules regarding bullying.
- Support the bullied child.
- Offer guidance to bystanders.
- Impose immediate consequences.
- Notify school team members and parents.
- Follow up and intervene as necessary.

ACTIVITY: DEALING WITH A BULLIES
WRITING PROMPT

1. What can you do to put a stop to the cycle of bullying?
2. How can you support your peers who have been bullied?
3. Do you think bullying is more prevalent online or in the classroom?
4. Do you think bullying is more prevalent at school or during extracurricular activities?
5. When you see someone being bullied, do you feel comfortable going to a school offical or adult for help?
6. What is the best way to get someone to stop bullying another person?
7. Have you ever talked to your parents about bullying? How did they respond?

12. BE ASSERTIVE WHEN COMMUNICATING WITH BULLIES

Assertive communication gives you ways to control your own responses to difficult bullying behavior. Being assertive is a core communication skill. Assertiveness shows that you respect yourself because you're willing to stand up for your interests and express your thoughts, feelings, and point of view, while also respecting the rights and beliefs of others. Assertive communication can help you control stress and anger when being victimized. Assertive communication enables you to express, both verbally and nonverbally, a wide range of feelings and thoughts, both positive and negative.

EXAMPLES OF ASSERTIVE COMMUNICATION
TYPICAL RESPONSE AFFECTIVE RESPONSE

Stop teasing Maia. It makes me uncomfortable when I hear you teasing Maia.

Talking during class is inappropriate. I am frustrated that you aren't listening to me.

You shouldn't do that. I feel sad when you say something like that to Andrew.

Sit down and be quiet. I get angry when you talk and joke during serious conversations.

I didn't want to see you hurt. I was shocked to see you fighting him, Shokha.

ADVANTAGES OF ASSERTIVE COMMUNICATION

- Assertiveness helps us feel good about ourselves and others.
- Assertiveness leads to the development of mutual respect with others.
- Assertiveness increases our self-esteem.
- Assertiveness helps us achieve our goals.
- Assertiveness minimizes hurting and alienating other people.
- Assertiveness reduces anxiety
- Assertiveness enables us to make decisions and free choices in life

EXAMPLE OF ASSERTIVE RESPONSE

Using "I" statements lets others know what you're thinking or feeling without sounding accusatory. For instance, say, "I disagree," rather than, "You're wrong." If you have a request, say "I would like you to help with this" rather than "You need to do this." Keep your requests simple and specific.

"I disagree with you. I see the situation this way."
"I would like you to respect my point of view."
"I feel offended by your remark."
"I didn't appreciate _____ (what you did, your tone of voice)."
"I would like for you to stop_____"
"No thank you, I'm not interested in _____"
"I really have to pay attention to this class lesson."

"That may be or may be not true, but I'm not interested at the moment."

"Thanks, but I'm not interested."

'Thanks, but I can't make that a priority right now."

"Thanks, but I need some time to myself right now."

"Thanks, but no thanks."

"Thanks for thinking of me, but I think I'll pass on this one."

"Thanks for keeping me in the loop, but I can't make it this time."

"Thank you for sharing, but I'd like to hear from other people in the group."

"I'll think about it and get back to you."

"I just don't know. Mind if I think about it for a while?"

ASSERTIVE RESPONSE ACTIVITY
BULLYING SCENARIOS

Cornish suggests that using scenarios as a projection analysis is an excellent predictor of violence (bullying) occurrences within a given organization's environment; Cornish also suggests that this aids the leadership in assessing or anticipating future climate trends. This activity invites the reader to read the following scenarios and apply assertive response "I" statements. The articulation of assertive "I" statements during a bullying occurrence protects victims and bystanders from being taken advantage of by others.

First Scenario

Lydia is a very popular and active student in school. She is in the tenth grade and maintains a 3.0 GPA; she is also captain of the school's dance team. Lydia and her friends were caught harassing another team member who is less popular, unattractive, and lacks dancing skills in comparison to the other team members. On one occasion, Lydia was overheard talking about the team member, saying how ugly she was. As the team member approached the group, Lydia proceeded to exclude her from the group by encouraging the other girls to walk away once the young lady approached.

Bully's response: When the teacher confronted the girls involved, they replied, "We were just having fun and joking around, weren't we?" The victim responded with a yes, and her face contorted into one of apparent disgust and annoyance.

Comment: Feinberg (2003) and Urbanski (2007) research suggest that the growth of adolescent girls into femininity consists of being more verbal in speaking their minds. This pattern also involves forming groups or cliques that generally consist of four to five friends who share a common interest. The incident highlights the rituals of bullying and how even academically excellent and involved students need corrective and instructive conversations as teachable moments that are grounded in the principles of social and emotional development.

Second Scenario

Brice has been at his school since preschool, but now he is in the seventh grade. The perception of Brice by others has been negative because of his history of fighting, being disruptive in class, and talking back to the teacher. Although Brice's behavior has improved, he is still viewed as a bully. On a day during the regular teacher's absence, Brice was walking to his seat when another classmate stuck his foot out, causing Brice to trip and fall.

At the time, the substitute teacher's back was turned, and therefore, the substitute did not witness the victimization. Brice immediately responded, and his first reaction was pushing the student back.

Comment: This incident highlights the rituals of bullying and how roles change depending on the situation. Although Brice's behavior usually identifies him as a bully, within this scenario he was the victim.

Third Scenario

Donald is in the eighth grade. He is much smaller than his other peers, including the girls. Donald is also quiet, and he tries hard to make friends by giving them gifts. Donald has been getting pushed around and teased since the beginning of the year, and he doesn't tell anyone, because he thinks that he would lose what he considers to be his friends. In January, another boy said Donald was walking too slowly as they were going to lunch, so the boy pushed him down.

Bully's response: The incident was immediately investigated by the school administration, and it included witnesses for both boys along with due process rights and parental contact. However, Donald (the victim) tried to justify the incident by saying, "We were just playing" (as if playing within the school's confines is not inappropriate).

The significance of these scenarios highlights how bullies verbally dodge taking ownership for their inappropriate action during school investigations of misconduct. Consequently, the bullies' abilities to maneuver around implicating investigations should be considered since students are frequently reluctant to report bullying behaviors to school administration, teachers, and parents for fear that nothing will be done or that it will make the situation worse. This is the victim's reality.

ACTIVITY

Create scenarios that capture your experience of being bullied

Write original incident	Rewrite as if original incident happened today: what would be the same or different
Emotional triggers	Emotional triggers
Your response	Your response
The outcome	The outcome

IMAGES OF ME (A PERSONAL REFLECTION ACTIVITY)!

SELF-AWARENESS

HELPS INDIVIUALS TO UNDERSTAND WHO THEY ARE AND THEREFORE VALIDATION FROM OTHERS MEAN NOTHING!

Self-awareness is the ability to accurately assess one's strengths and limitations, with a well-grounded sense of confidence and a growth mindset. The components of self-awareness include the following:

- Identification of emotions
- Accurate self- perception
- Recognition of strengths
- Self-confidence
- Self-efficacy

WRITING AND DRAWING PROMPT

WHO ARE YOU! Are you the individual that the bully describes? **NO, YOU'RE NOT!** Choose an aspect of your identity such as your accurate self-perception, outward or inner beauty, athletic ability, self-confidence, or mental toughness for the activity images of you writing and drawing reflection prompt.

_____

_____

_____

BLANK PAGE FOR DRAWING PROMPT ACTIVITY

BLANK PAGE FOR DRAWING PROMPT ACTIVITY

_____

_____

_____

_____

_____

_____

_____

_____

_____

_____

_____

_____

_____

_____

_____

_____

_____

_____

ACTIVITY: GETTING TO KNOW YOU!
SELF-AWARENESS QUESTIONNAIRE

NOTE: Select one answer A or B for each number based on your own perception.

1. A) I tend to tell people what is on my mind.
   B) I tend to keep things to myself.

2. A) I see myself as cool and guarded with others.
   B) I see myself as warm and friendly with others.

3. A) I tend to show my emotions to others.
   B) I tend to keep my emotions inside.

4. A) I see myself as fast-paced.
   B) I see myself as slow-paced.

5. A) I see myself as a risk-taker in most situations.
   B) I view myself as one who avoids or minimizes risk in most situations.

6. A) I see myself as playful and fun-loving.
   B) I see myself as serious and thoughtful.

7. A) I tend to wait for others to initiate interaction with me.
   B) I tend to initiate interactions.

8. A) I tend to talk in terms of opinions.
   B) I tend to talk in terms of facts.

9. A) I tend to like to work with others.
   B) I tend to like to work alone.

10. A) I tend to take charge of a situation.
    B) I tend to remain in the background.

11. A) I see myself as outgoing and direct.
    B) I see myself as quiet and moderate.

12. A) I tend to focus on the outcome and results.
    B) I tend to focus on the process or the method.

13. BULLYING VICTIMIZATION WARNING SIGNS

There are many warning signs that may indicate that someone is affected by bullying—either being bullied or bullying others. Recognizing the warning signs is an important first step in acting against bullying. Not all children who are bullied or are bullying others ask for help.

BULLYING STATICTICS

- Adults only intercept 11–15 percent of bullying incidents.
- 85 percent of bullying incidents occur without interventions.
- One out of four students are bullied.
- Every seven minutes a child is bullied.

- 280,000 students are attacked monthly.
- 3.2 million children are bullied every year.
- Every day 160,000 students avoid school because of being bullied.
- 100,000 children carry guns to school each year.
- Bullied victims are two to nine times more likely to consider suicide.

BULLYING WARNING SIGNS

Exclusion from social activities	Acts of retaliation
Frequent sick days	Change in appetite
Sudden withdrawal or isolation as well avoidance	Difficulty sleeping, loss of sleep, or nightmares
Feelings of helplessness / depression	Unexplained injuries
Tendency to self-harm, or suicide ideation	Suffering grades or lack of interest in school
Missing or destroyed personal property	Supression of events

It is important to talk with children who show signs of being bullied or bullying others. These warning signs can also point to other issues or problems, such as depression or substance abuse. Talking to the child can help identify the root of the problem.

14. INTERVENTIONS FOR BULLYING AND SCHOOL VIOLENCE

BULLYING RESOLUTION MODEL

*NOTE: The diagrams representing the Bullying Resolution Model highlight one model consisting of five driving forces for each cycle that uniquely contribute to the resolutions.

The Bullying Resolution Model (see diagram below) is a comprehensive five-cycle approach that promotes conflict de-escalation, and resolution. The model components consist of five driving forces embedded within the five bullying cycles purposefully designed to achieve a resolution.

56 | THE BULLYING PHENOMENOM: Breaking the Cycle

1. Bullying Roles
2. Bullying Type
3. Collaborative Involvement
4. Instructive, Corrective, and Intervention
5. New Skill Acquisition

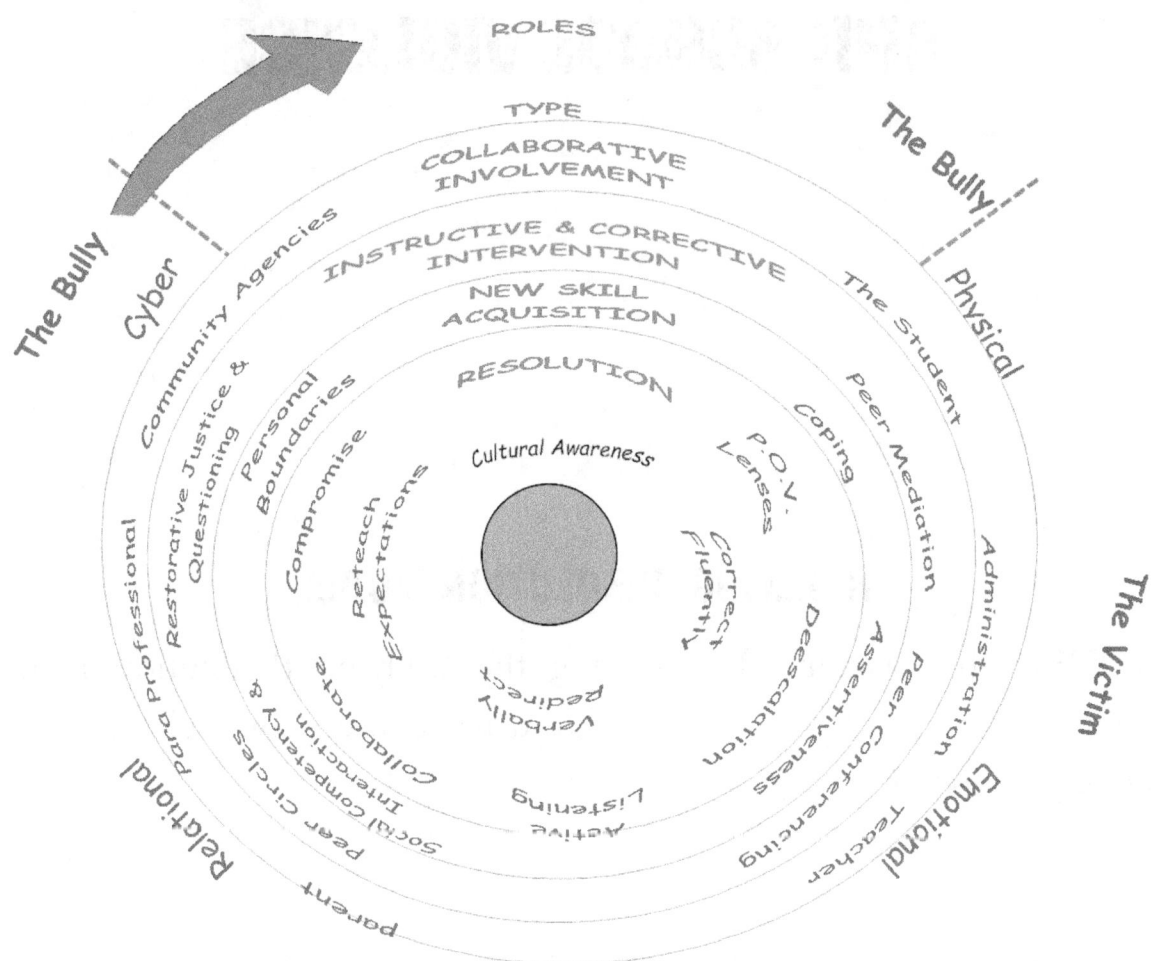

The Bullying Resolution Model's five-cycle components can address multilevel conflicts ranging from minor inappropriateness to severe or complex dilemmas.

14. INTERVENTIONS FOR BULLYING AND SCHOOL VIOLENCE | 57

- Aid the facilitator in confronting the bully, victim, and bystander to seek reconciliation
- Aid the facilitator and conflicted parties to identify the problem, select best alternatives, monitor setbacks, and evaluate progress until a resolution takes hold during as well as after the process
- When two or more driving forces are maneuvered, the facilitator will obtain a greater resolution.

NOTE: *The facilitator assumes the role of the monitor, directing, being supportive, encouraging participation, and giving encouragement while the conflicted parties collaborate until the resolution is realized.*

BULLYING ROLES AND RESOLUTION CYCLE

Let's put first things first! The *bullying roles and resolution component* (see diagram 1) function are the initial cycle of the model but only after de-escalation of angered parties has occurred.

IDENTIFY TRIGGERS THAT DE-ESCALATE OR ESCALATE CONFLICTS

Triggers that surface during conflict are simply a stimulus that evokes feelings of emotional upsets, which may lead to inappropriate behaviors. Often, our triggers are experiences, situations, or stressors that unconsciously remind us of past traumas, feelings of sadness, anxiety, or panic. Every human has triggers that they must learn to self-regulate. The challenge is learning to identify our triggers and then recognizing them, especially when negative interactions occur because we must choose our responses, which are direct correlations of growth.

DE-ESCALLATION VS. ESCALATION TRIGGERS

- Take Ownership / Aggression
- Have Integrity / Lack of Fairness
- Eyecontact / Identity Management
- Conversational Tone / Voice Incompetence
- Active Listening / Relationship Threats
- Show Empathy / Lack of Seif-Regulation
- Manage Thoughts / Emotions/ Being Falsely Accused
- Response / Unforegiveness

ACTIVITY: WHICH CONFLICT ESCALATOR TRIGGERS ME?

NOTE: How would you plot each conflict escalator on the scale? Ask yourself, which conflict escalator triggers me, with zero being the lowest, and ten being the highest level of frustration.

LOWEST MIDDLE HIGHEST

0 ++ 10

BULLDOZING

Using aggressive behavior such as intimidating another person by falsely accusing, running over, name-calling, shouting, swearing, threatening, and taunting.

CONFLICT ARCHEOLOGY

Bringing up past failures, wrongdoings, and unrealized promises.

PUT-DOWNS

Using words, body language, disguised humor, posture, gazes, gestures, and name-calling to insult another.

GLOBAL STATEMENTS

Using global words that are accusatory in nature to blame or insult others like *you, always, never, and every time.*

COUNTERATTACK

Attacking the other person by throwing back insulting comments instead of listening to the other's point of view to solve the problem.

ABOVE IT ALL

Acting superior or high minded towards other person without listening to viewpoints concerning the issue. The Above-It-All person's mental state only supports the notion I'm better, this is beneath me, and dealing with you is petty.

SILENT TREATMENT

Avoiding the person, denying the problem ever happened, hoping it goes away, or is not reported.

ACTIVITY: BEHAVIOR REFLECTION FORM

What happened?
_____
_____
_____

Who was involved?
_____
_____
_____

What were the reasons?
_____
_____
_____

How do I feel (circle best choice)?
_____
_____
_____

MAD UPSET SAD SCARED FRUSTRATED CONFUSED JEALOUS LONELY

Why wasn't this acceptable behavior?

_____
_____
_____
_____

What could I have done instead?

_____
_____
_____
_____

What will I do the next time I feel this way?

_____
_____
_____
_____

14. INTERVENTIONS FOR BULLYING AND SCHOOL VIOLENCE | 63

1. BULLYING ROLES AND RESOLUTION CYCLE DIAGRAM

The resolution component determines how in-depth a dialogue should be in resolving the conflict that caused the problem (Identifying the problem).

64 | THE BULLYING PHENOMENOM: Breaking the Cycle

The bullying role determines which students are the bullies, the victims, and the bystanders (Define the problem). Through investigation and restorative questioning the facilitator can identify who initiated the conflict, the nature of conflict, and the role each person assumed.

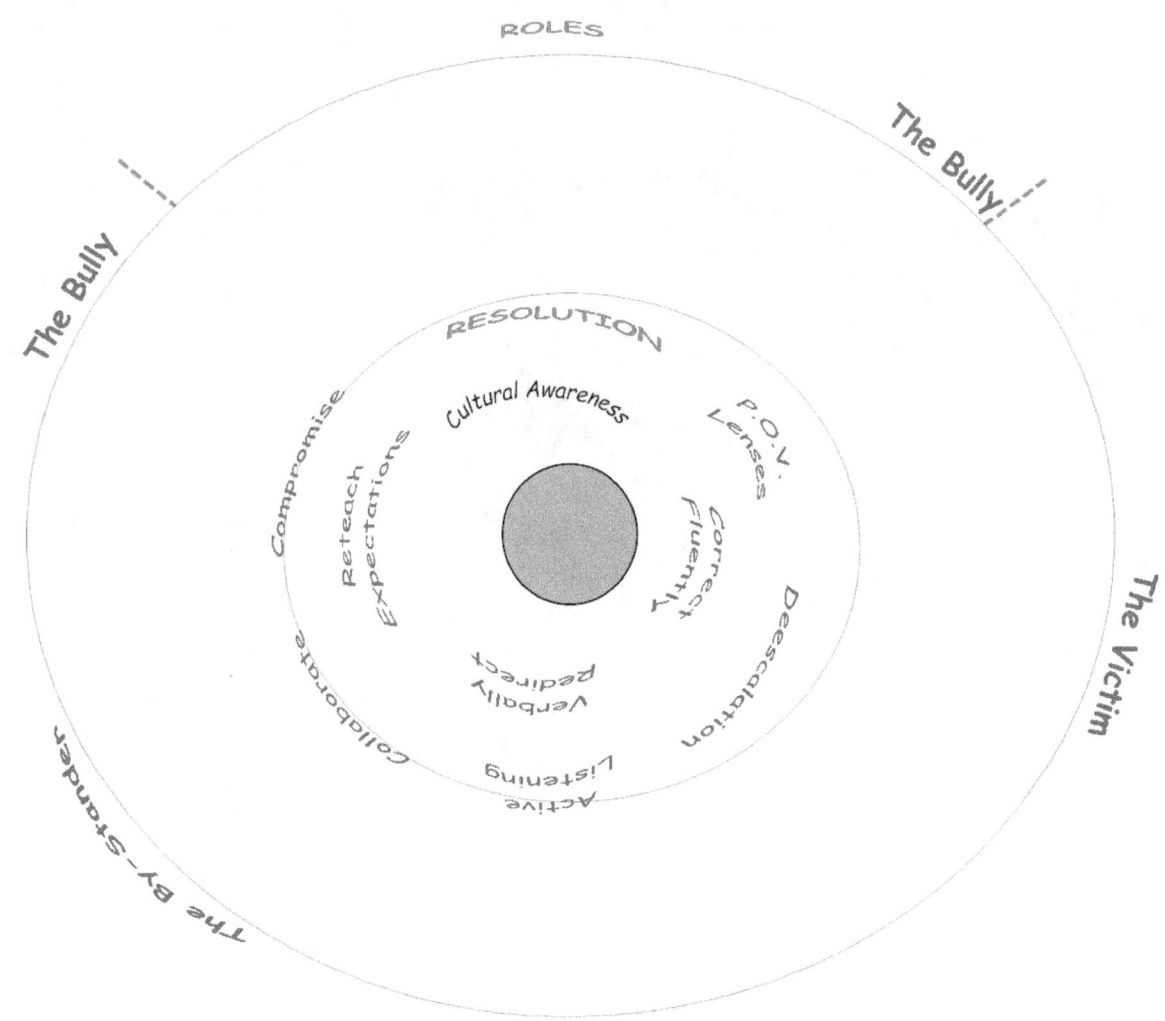

14. INTERVENTIONS FOR BULLYING AND SCHOOL VIOLENCE | 65

ACTIVITY: PROBLEM SOLVING MATRIX

NOTE: *The activity requirement will guide you through the problem-solving process. Use scenarios that you created in the prior activity.*

IDENTIFY THE PROBLEM

THINK OF SEVERAL SOLUTIONS		

EXAMINE THE PROS AND CONS OF THE SOLUTION					
Pros	Cons	Pros	Cons	Pros	Cons

CHOOSE A SOLUTION

66 | THE BULLYING PHENOMENOM: Breaking the Cycle

BULLYING TYPE AND RESOLUTION CYCLE

The second driving force (see diagram 2) of the bullying resolution cycle focus on identifying the bullying type (see diagram below) (physical, emotional, relational, or cyber).

2. BULLYING TYPE AND RESOLUTION CYCLE DIAGRAM

This driving force identifies which medium was utilized in victimizing another; this cycle helps to further define part of the problem.

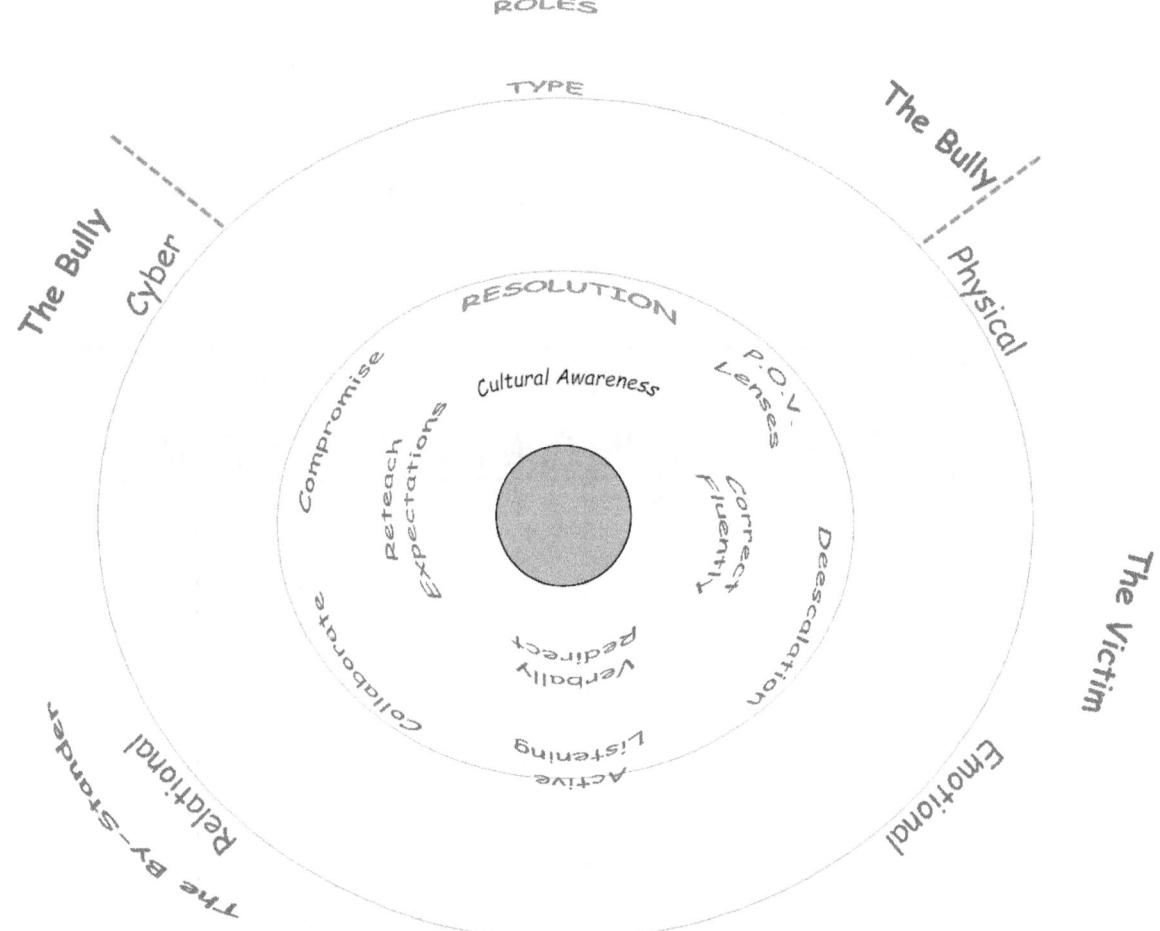

ACTIVITY: WHAT TYPE OF LISTENER ARE YOU?
SELF- EVALUATION SCALE

Listening Evaluation Statements	Excellent	Good	Some-What	Poor
I Look at the Person Who Is Talking to Me.				
I Think About What the Person Is Saying.				
I Use Facial Expressions to Show that I Am Interested.				
I Listen to, Understand, and then Speak to Be Understood.				
I Stop Myself from Interrupting While Others Are Speaking.				

68 | THE BULLYING PHENOMENOM: Breaking the Cycle

COLLABORATIVE INVOLVEMENT CYCLE

The third driving force (see diagram 3) in the bully resolution cycle focus on collaborative involvement (Generating alternatives solution). The community collaborative involvement phase identifies the school's learning community's internal and/or external resources to bring about change. For a resolution to take hold among conflicted students, they must be involved collaboratively in the problem-solving process.

3. COLLABORATIVE INVOLVEMENT CYCLE DIAGRAM

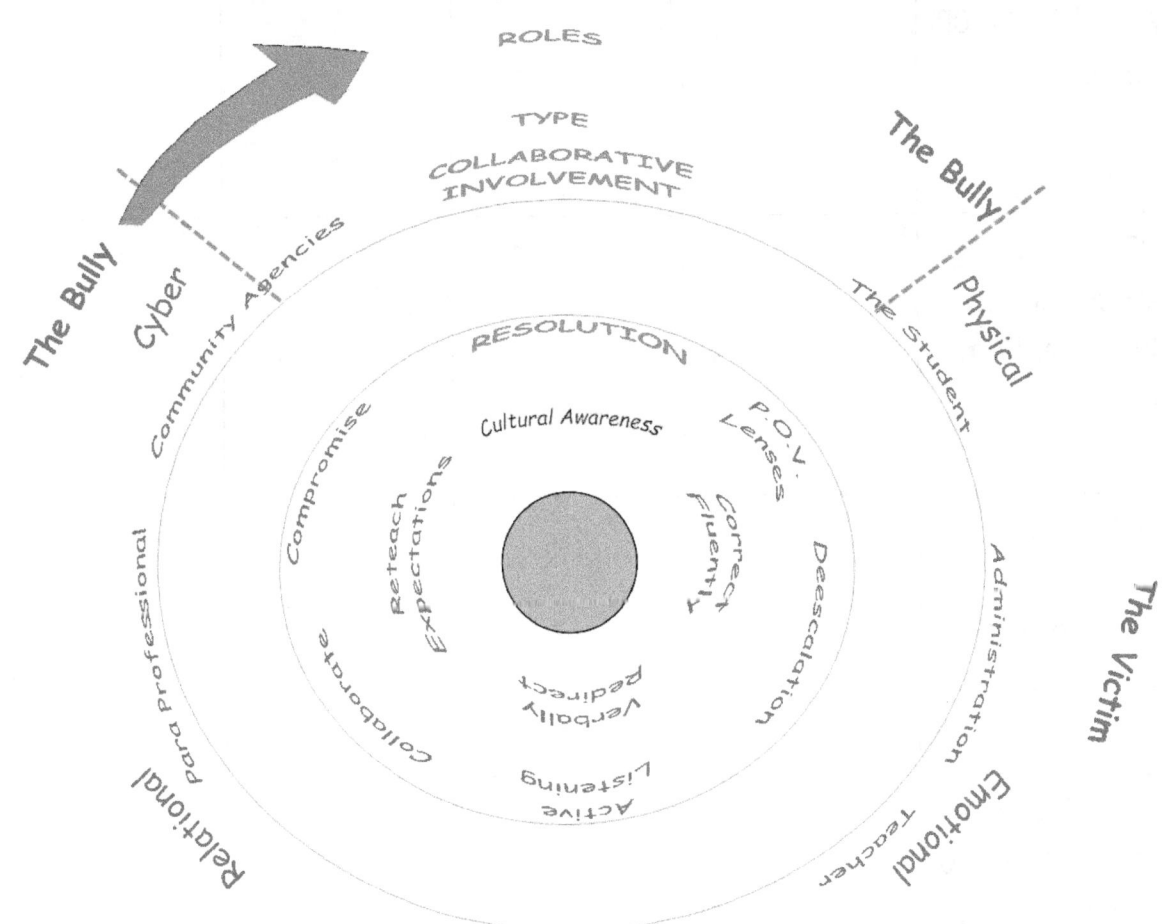

This consists of generating alternative solution through collaborative dialogue and evaluating and selecting the best alternatives until a restorative posture is realized. An internal community involvement team should include the students, teachers, administrators, parents, counselors, and paraprofessionals.

An external community involvement team should include agencies such as faith-based organizations, social services, mental health organizations, and mentoring organizations. The collaborative facilitators illustrating, modeling, coaching, and generating conflict alternatives, as well as correlating to the learning communities, behavior expectations will empower and encourage students to make better choices, self-manage, and take ownership when conflicts occur in the absence of an adult.

RESTORATIVE QUESTIONS THAT RESPOND TO CHALLENGING BEHAVIOR

- What happened?
- Where did it take place?
- What were you thinking of at the time?
- What have you thought about since?
- Who was involved?
- Who saw or heard?
- Who has been affected by what you have done?
- In what way have they been affected?
- What do you think you need to do to make things right?

RESTORATIVE QUESTIONS THAT HELP THOSE HARMED BY OTHER'S ACTIONS

- What did you think when you realized what had happened?
- What impact has this incident had on you and others?
- What has been the hardest thing for you?
- What do you think needs to happen to make things right? (International Institute for Restorative Practices)

INSTRUCTIVE AND CORRECTIVE CYCLE

Generating alternative solutions and implementing achievable (see diagram 4) actions toward resolutions highlights the fourth driving force in the bully resolution cycle—focus on instructive and corrective responses. As a behavioral response, corrective action affords the opportunity for the student to demonstrate and practice the expected behavior as a replacement for the inappropriate behavior.

4. INSTRUCTIVE AND CORRECTIVE CYCLE DIAGRAM

Restorative practice goals are to build relationships, be accountable for self and others, build social and emotional skills, and create positive solutions to repair harm. As a result, instructive responses should be used when the student's inappropriate behavior is caused by a lack of knowledge or the student does not know the desired behavior expectation. Corrective responses should be used when the student knows behavior expectations but disregards climate norms.

5. ACQUISITION OF NEW SKILLS CYCLE

The fifth and final driving force in the bully resolution cycle focuses on acquisition of new skills (see diagram 5). This driving force provides opportunities for the participating parties in conflict to acquire alternative skills in dealing with issues.

ACTIVITY: GET ORGANIZED
WORD SEARCH

```
O R G A N I Z A T I O N O O I
C I T I Z E N S H I P G M N O
N O I T A I T O G E N N O N C
N O I T A R E P O O C I Y O S
E C N E U L F N I E T V I I R
T E R I S E N G M A I L E T O
W H Y E O L N P C Y A O T A T
O E S N A I A I W B P S E V U
R I I I R T N R O P R M E O R
K E R A H U I R A T U E M N I
I O H Y M I A V A M R I S N N
N S D M L T T Y I I E B N I E
G N O M I O M M F T L O M E H
C C E O H A W I O A Y R B D O
S I N Y T I I I B A T P A D A
```

WORD LIST

Citizenship	Empathy	Organization
Collaboration	Influence	Problem solving
Communication	Innovation	Sharing
Cooperation	Negotiation	Adaptability
Creativity	Networking	

74 | THE BULLYING PHENOMENOM: Breaking the Cycle

ACQUISITION OF NEW SKILLS CYCLE DIAGRAM

ROLES

- The Bully
- The Bully
- The By-Stander
- The Student

TYPE
- Cyber
- Physical
- Emotional
- Relational

COLLABORATIVE INVOLVEMENT
- Community Agencies
- Para professional
- Parent
- Teacher
- Administration
- Peer Mediation

INSTRUCTIVE & CORRECTIVE INTERVENTION
- Restorative Justice & Questioning
- Peer Circles
- Social Competency & Interaction
- Active Listening
- Assertiveness
- Peer Conferencing
- Coping

NEW SKILL ACQUISITION
- Personal Boundaries
- Compromise
- Reteach Expectations
- Collaborate
- Verbally Redirect
- Deescalation
- P.O.V. Lenses
- Correct Fluently

RESOLUTION
- Cultural Awareness

This process helps students take ownership and see the humanity of others. At this point, the facilitator and involved parties can sense internal emotional and mental changes taking hold and beginning to effect change within the resolution outcome.

POINT OF VIEW

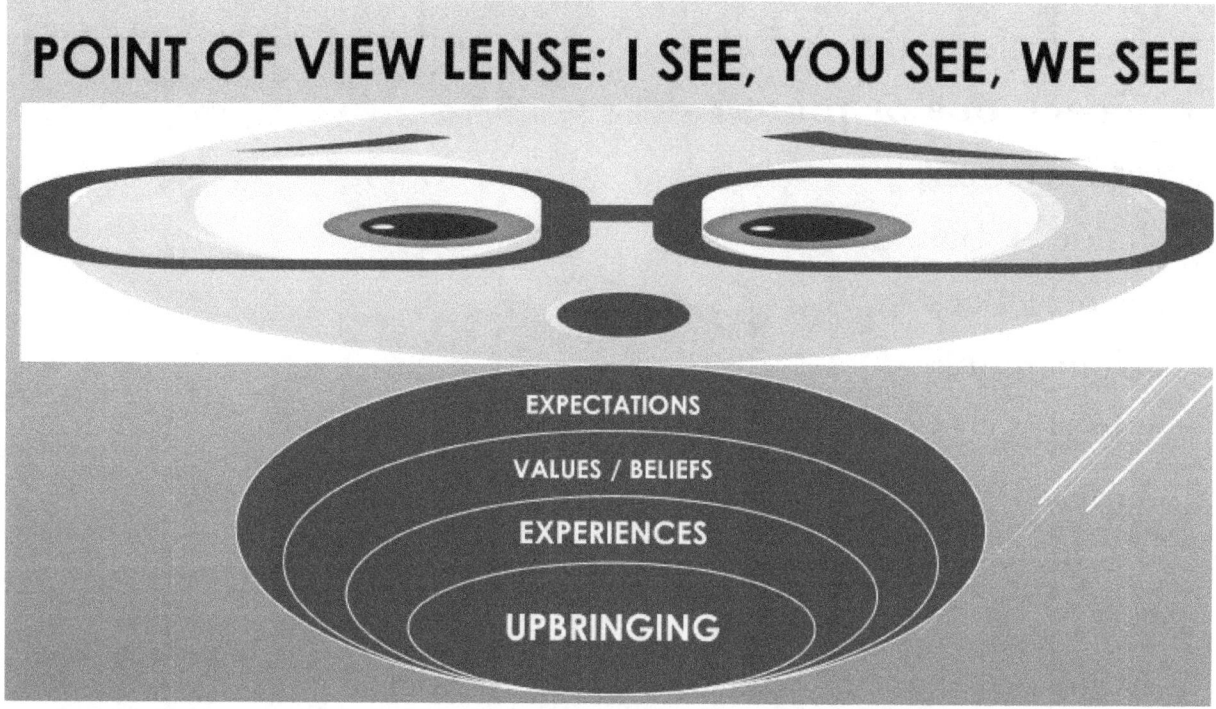

These driving forces contribute to student skill building that support resolution outcomes. The conflicted parties are encouraged to engage collaboratively in social interaction through discussions. This process encourages active listening, shared viewpoints of the conflict, feelings, and potential compromises.

POINT OF VIEW REFLECTIONS:

1. **In this conflict, what was your point of view based on (check one or more)?**
   Expectations
   Values / Beliefs
   Experiences
   Upbringing
   Needs
   Goals
   Feelings / Emotions

2. Who was the other person in this conflict?
   _____
   _____
   _____

3. Did you and the conflicted party explain your point of view extensively?
   _____
   _____
   _____

4. Which point of view attribute do you think the conflicted party's point of view was based on (check one or more)?
   Expectations
   Values / Beliefs
   Experiences
   Upbringing
   Needs
   Goals
   Feelings/ Emotions

5. As you reflect on the conflict now, how might the other person's point of view alter your own?

   _____
   _____
   _____

BRIDGING RELATIONSHIPS

Also, during these sessions, the facilitator utilizes prompts in moving the social and emotional growth forward, climate expectations, conflict de-escalation, coping mechanisms, assertiveness in addressing perpetrators, uniqueness, and similarities and differences that bridge relationships.

POINT OF VIEW ACTIVITY

I SEE! UNIQUE DIFFERENCES	*WE SEE!* SIMILARITIES	*YOU SEE!* UNIQUE DIFFERENCES

15. COPING STRATEGIES FOR EMOTIONAL MANAGEMENT

Coping mechanisms are skills we all have that allow us to make sense of our negative experiences and integrate them into a healthy, sustainable perspective of the world. When life gives us issues or problems to solve, our coping skills help us to deal with and attempt to overcome life difficulties.

COPING STRATEGIES

1. Take deep breaths
2. Do a positive activity
3. Think of something funny
4. Play sports
5. Take a quick walk
6. Practice yoga
7. Stand up and stretch
8. Listen to music

9. Take a time out
10. Slowly count to ten
11. Talk to a friend
12. Talk to an adult
13. Say, "I can do this."
14. Read a good book
15. Set a goal
16. Jog in place
17. Write in a journal
18. Hum your favorite song
19. Doodle on paper
20. Draw a picture
21. Use positive self-talk
22. Visualize your favorite place
23. Meditate
24. Use a stress ball
25. Dance
26. Write a letter
27. Chew gum
28. Paint your nails
29. Write a story
30. Blog
31. Read a joke book
32. Write a poem
33. Drink cold water
34. Clean Something
35. Look at pictures you've taken

15. COPING STRATEGIES FOR EMOTIONAL MANAGEMENT | 81

ACTIVITY: IDENTIFYING COPING SKILLS

NOTE: See if you can find the following strategies written backwards, then write them on the lines below.

1. KNIHT FO A LUFECAEP ECALP. __ __ __ __ __ __ __ __
   __ __ __ __ __ __ __ __
   __ __ __ __ __ .

2. EKAT EERHT PEED SHTAERB __ __ __ __ __ __ __ __ __
   __ __ __ __
   __ __ __ __ __ __

3. ESNET DNA XALER RUOY SELCSUM. __ __ __ __ __ __ __ __
   __ __ __ __ __ __ __ __ __
   __ __ __ __ __ __ __ .

4. ESICREXE. __ __ __ __ __ __ __ __ .

CONCLUSION

According to the U.S. Department of Health & Human Services, approximately 1 in 4 U.S. students say they've experienced in-school bullying, and about 30 percent of young people say they've bullied others. As an intervention the author's Bullying Resolution Model uses a solution driven design to provide classroom leaders with the tools to successfully intervene and manage bullying situations as well as deter the victimization of others.

CONCLUSION

REFERENCES

Allen, K. P. 2010a. "A bullying intervention system: Reducing risk and creating support for aggressive students." *Preventing School Failure* 54, 199–209, http://dx.doi.org/10.1080/10459880903496289.

Allen, K. P. 2010b. "Classroom management, bullying, and teacher practices. *Professional Educator* 34(1), 1–15, http://www.theprofessionaleducator.org/.

American Educational Research Association. 2013. "Prevention of bullying in schools, colleges, and universities." Research Report and Recommendations, Washington, D.C.

Bowllan, N. M. 2011. "Implementation and evaluation of a comprehensive, school wide bullying prevention program in an urban/suburban middle school." *Journal of School Health* 81, 167–73, http://dx.doi.org/10.1111/j.1746-1561.2010.00576.x.

Caselman, T. D. (2005). Stop and think: An impulse control program in a school setting. *School Social Work Journal, 30*(1), 40.

Cook, C. R., et al. 2010. "Predictors of bullying and victimization in childhood and adolescence: A meta-analytic investigation." *School Psychology Quarterly* 25, 65–83. doi:10.1037/a0020149.

Cottello, J. M. 2008. "Bullying in schools: Identification, prevention, and intervention." Master's thesis, WorldCat, OCLO no. 299755599).

"Cyberbullying: A growing problem." 2010. *Science Daily,* http://www.sciencedaily.com/releases/2010/02/100222104939.htm.

Dake, J. A., Price, J. H., and Telljohann, S. K. 2003. "The nature and extent of bullying at school." *Journal of School Health* 73, 173–80, http://dx.doi.org/10.1111/j.1746-1561.2003.tb03599.x.

Feinberg, T. 2003. "Bullying prevention and intervention." *Principal Leadership* 4(1), 10-14.

Frank, J. (2013). Raising Cultural Awareness in the English Language Classroom. In *English teaching forum* (Vol. 51, No. 4, p. 2). US Department of State. Bureau of Educational and Cultural Affairs, Office of English Language Programs, SA-5, 2200 C Street NW 4th Floor, Washington, DC 20037.

McKinney, B. C., Kimsey, W. D., & Fuller, R. M. (1995). *Mediator communication competencies: Interpersonal communication and alternative dispute resolution.* Burgess International.

Meyer-Adams, N., and Conner, B. 2008. "School violence: Bullying behaviors and the psychosocial school environment in middle schools." *Children and Schools* 30, 211–221, http://dx.doi.org/10.1093/cs/30.4.211.

Neiman, S. 2011. "Crime, violence, discipline, and safety in US public schools: 2009–10" (NCES 2011–320), http://nces.ed.gov/pubs2011/2011320.pdf.

Ogle, D. M. (1986). KWL: A teaching model that develops active reading of expository text. *Reading teacher.*

Ruffin, D. (2017). *The Bullying Phenomenon: Breaking the Cycle.* WestBow Press.

Urbanski, J. 2007. "The relationship between school connectedness and bullying victimization in secondary students. PhD diss., ProQuest, UMI no. 3306896.

US Department of Health and Human Services, Office of Adolescent Health. 2013. "Bullying," http://www.hhs.gov/ash/oah/adolescent-health-topics/healthy-relationships/bullying.html.

ADDITIONAL RESOURCES

1. AntiBullying Network http://antibullying.net/resourceswwwlinks.htm

2. American Psychological Association http://www.apa.org

3. Cyberbullying http://www.ncpc.org/topics/cyberbullying

4. National Bullying Prevention Center
   http://www.pacer.org/bullying/resources

5. Stop Bullying http://wwwstopbullying.gov/index.html

6. Substance abuse and mental health services administration
   https://www.samhsa.gov/tribal-ttac/resources/bullying

7. The Bullying Phenomenon Breaking the Cycle
   http://www.bullyphenomenon.com
   http://www.westbowpress.com

www.ingramcontent.com/pod-product-compliance
Lightning Source LLC
Chambersburg PA
CBHW060426010526
44118CB00017B/2377